BODY LANGUAGE EXPOSED

BY

Daryo Nagari

* * *

Copyright

Disclaimer

The author and publisher of this book have used all reasonable effort in its preparation. We make no representation or warranty in respect of accuracy. Application, fitness for purpose or completeness of the content herein.

The information contained is strictly for entertainment purposes only. Any person applying any ideas proposed within this publication does so at their own discretion and risk.

BEAUTIFUL GAME 179

Introduction

Charlie Chaplin, Buster Keaton, in fact all those wonderful stars of the silent movies had no other means of communication but their body language and facial expression. Except of course for the occasional text bubble.

Yet they could convey any message they needed to. They could tell an entire story without speaking.

They used these expressions in overt exaggerated form in order that the audience were in no doubt as to the message being sent. The responsibility was on them to do a good job

In everyday life, conversation and communication, the language of the body is much more subtle. Therefore the responsibility is upon the reader to decipher correctly what is being left unsaid.

Long before the silent movies non verbal communication was an important survival tool message from affection to aggression and everything in between were conveyed using this method alone. We would have been experts at reading the tiniest signal from other humans.

Once we started talking the skill became less and less used and dulled, until today it is only usually recognised at a unconscious level.

This book aims to help you re-sharpen those skills, to bring body language back into the conscious realm.

Using observation to once again see what is being said to us by another person.

To bring our instinctive feelings about other people and what they are really trying to tell us back under our control.

Practice looking for tell tale signs and use the information in this book to put yourself in charge.

Ensure you are sending the right messages to others use your own body to best affect situations and how you are perceived by those around you.

Non Verbal communication

This is everything we tell others about a situation, our emotional state and our intention, that does not come from the words we say.

This is all about the messages we convey to others and they to us via our body language our gestures and our facial expression and the inflection in the tone of our voices.

All the things we communicate to each other at a primal level except the actual words that come out of our mouths.

So how do those messages come across to us all?

A whopping fifty five percent of message projection and reception is through body language alone.

This is our stance our proximity to others as well as our movements, posture, positioning of our feet and hands too.

As well as these body positions are our facial expression and the changes that take place in each of these in response to various stimuli.

We call them expressions because they are an outward visible expression of the invisible emotion being experienced by a person.

On top of all that there are micro expressions. A micro expression is the same as any other facial expression except it occurs in a fraction of a second.

They happen without us even realising that they have occurred. Micro expressions are completely honest unconscious responses telling us the emotional state of a subject without any conscious interference.

Micro expressions are usually 'masked' within a half a second. That is unless of course the person has nothing to hide!

Next coming into the frame is how we say something to another human being, our tone of voice which constitutes a further thirty eight percent.

In all that's a staggering ninety three percent of our communication has nothing whatsoever to do with what we actually say.

If you've done your math correctly you will notice that leaves a poultry seven percent of communication left to what we are actually saying.

This leads us to the natural assumption that the least honest part of any communication is in fact the actual verbalised words!

In future when you have a conversation with somebody remember these figures and don't get sucked into believing what you are told.

In the same breath remember to present yourself properly to others. The signals you send out are received at a unconscious level by others.

Any parents among you will instinctively know that the figures above are correct. You know your children so well that if they try to tell you something which is not true you can 'feel' it.

You know when they are uncomfortable or happy they don't have to tell you feel it.

What of course is happening is you are relying on the non verbal without even realising it.

Because we receive these non verbal signals at a unconscious level it sometimes confuses even ourselves. Often we will comment that we may like or dislike someone when we hardly know them, or even on first meeting them.

This instinctive reading is fine but can easily be clouded, especially if you are dealing with an accomplished liar who is very adept at masking their emotions.

Look at politicians. They are human but when they communicate they contrive their expressions and body movements to project what they want to project. If you want to see what a politician really thinks you will have to become a master at reading micro expression!

Whilst on the subject of politicians it is worth mentioning this about verbal communication.

Although it accounts for only seven percent of all communication, politicians, salesmen and all manner of others even use this against us.

In an effort to maximise their influence they use language and language patterns which are subliminal. They use what we call embedded commands to influence our thinking. so watch out for these slippery b*st*rds.

Once you have read this book I suggest you take a look at footage of Richard Nixon in the last days of his Presidency of the United States.

What he says is completely at odds with his body language and his micro expressions. He has lost everything and has forgotten himself, he is relying on his words only and the rest of him is letting him down.

See how many times he pokes his tongue out at the American people and does the 'I've got a secret' tongue jut during these speeches and interviews.

If we want to make the most of reading non verbal communications then we need to make a conscious effort to decipher them.

When we make a concerted conscious effort to read these signals it is amazing how much more you will understand the messages that are being screamed out by others.

Imagine once you have honed your non verbal reading skills to be second nature then reading other people will become instinctive, you will have that same feeling about others as you do with your children or others who are particularly close to you. Friends, salesmen, work colleagues. Never be conned or outwitted again.

Before moving onto the actual 'reads' or 'tells' as they are called let's get some background then we can look at what you need to do to be able to see things more clearly, in order to become an expert in the reading of non verbal communication.

Also from now on in this book I will be referring to 'subjects' and 'readers'. The reader is you and your subject the person whose non verbal communications you are trying to decipher.

Congruence

This is the matching of what our body 'says' or projects and how we put the message across to what we say verbally.

All three should be giving the same message.

Message harmony makes others feel comfortable and safe and we feel the same when we witness this congruence ourselves. Congruence in communication is the key to trust and rapport.

Congruence can also be a visual only read. For instance are the body signals matching the expression on the face? The body could be in an aggressive stance and the facial expression calm.

If that is the case you may have missed a telling micro expression of aggressiveness which was subsequently covered by deliberately held facial expression, perhaps to draw you in under false pretext.

Whenever communicating we are looking for congruence to reinforce the spoken word

Incongruence

The opposite of congruence.

The mismatching of what is projected by our body signals with both how we are saying something and what is actually said. Incongruence is discomfort.

I briefly mentioned masking in the previous chapter; masking is the act of literally hiding our true feelings. We deliberately use posture and facial expressions to portray a false emotional state.

One thing about masking is that it often causes incongruence because it is in conflict with the genuine feeling of the subject. Some people are good at these masking, our previously mentioned politicians for example.

There is something very important to remember about masking with regard to facial expression.

That is that masking occurs after a micro expression and not before. So a true emotional state will be visible for a split second right before the masking.

A subject who is angered but does not want to let on will show a minute sign of this anger right before masking it with a disarming smile.

* * *

The mind

How we behave is governed by our mind or should I say minds.

There are the things we chose to do at any given time. This behaviour is being controlled by the conscious mind.

Concentration and task orientated it applies all its thinking power to achieving its goal. The conscious mind can only hold one thought at a time.

Then there are things we do habitually. These habits are controlled by the unconscious. Once we have performed a task often enough consciously and we become proficient at it. It is assigned to the unconscious as a learned habit, we then do it automatically. Habits can be good or bad.

So we learn how to drive a car by making conscious effort in the early days and after a certain time has passed and experience gained the unconscious takes over the mundane parts of the job. If you have ever updated your car you may have experienced your unconscious habits working against you.

When you first start to drive your new car you are so used to say flicking the indicator or turn signal switch on one side of the column that you keep attempting to do it for a while, even though it is on the other side of the column in your new car.

In fact sometimes there is slight panic when we attempt to hit the switch and it's not there or the wipers come on!

At that point we have to bring our concentration to bear for a second while we figure out why the unconscious is alarmed.

Bad habits are formed in exactly the same way. Ask any smoker.

Initially due to peer pressure or some other reason conscious effort had to be made to light up and put up with the disgusting taste in the mouth and the feelings of nausea or dizziness,

Once the task had been performed enough times it becomes automatic and worse still linked to other activities. So you see the unconscious operates all the time but it is not necessarily working in our best interests

Finally there are the things we do instinctively, things we have no control over whatsoever. This instinctive mind is the part that controls our non verbal communications.

It takes care of the fundamentals like breathing the things that keep us alive as an animal. One of the ways it has always kept us alive and well is by protecting us from threats. It does things instinctively.

Long ago, for our ancestors the threats were very severe and very real, predators everywhere. This ancestral or limbic part of our brain built in automatic defence mechanisms to cope with survival.

This part of the brain, only deals in two absolutes, fear and pleasure. It thinks in black and white.

Whenever we experience either fear or pleasure the limbic or ancestral brain reacts instantly through non verbal signals, non verbals do not lie, they simply do not have time to. They are immediate and 'instinctive'

To understand them a little better we need to understand the fundamentals handed down from our ancestors.

You have probably heard the expression fight or flight, well this is only half the story these are the two last resorts but there are other things that occur before we get to the last resorts.

What actually happens is there is a scary or worrying situation, when we spot this we tend to freeze, then we get ready to or actually run away or flee then finally there is the turn and fight. This is dealt with in detail next.

attempt to put distance between ourselves and the threat.

Fourth

When all other options are exhausted we turn face our attacker and fight. Or at least we prepare to.

In this day and age we don't generally have to worry about wild beasts and as the threat has become watered down by modern society so too has our need to use the fright, freeze, flight and fight mechanisms,

Instead of fear and pleasure we are more likely to encounter comfort or discomfort on a daily basis.

The reactions are virtually the same except this initial input could be anything which makes us uncomfortable.

So the initial fright is now modified into anything which causes us to feel uncomfortable. The stimuli can be internal as well as external. So we may have a thought we may see or hear something which causes this gut reaction.

During these watered down versions of the freeze reaction we may do a full body freeze or more likely a modified version like a partial freeze, and instead of having to wait for the danger to pass as with our predator we may only do a micro freeze.

This may even be in the form of a facial expression such as the freezing of an open mouth. The freeze gives us time to catch up and assess, if things are fine then we carry on.

The next stage in the process has also modified itself from the full flight from the predator to making ready for flight; we can show this intention to go in many ways. Distancing is a very common one standing away or even just leaning away is an attempt to distance ourselves from the 'threat'. So too is the way we face our feet and even sometimes mimic walking or running actions by shuffling our feet or moving our legs.

Finally the fight. Once again, toned down to fit into socially acceptable behaviour. Notice when someone has become very upset with the input they have received, they will stand firm puff their bodies up like a grand old silverback. Often again the feet may kick out in a symbolically aggressive action.

When we are relaxed and content or inputs are pleasing everything about our body language and expressions are relaxed.

So we can see that the modern equivalent of Fear or happy, Is actually comfort or discomfort. And once you know what to look for you will become an expert at reading the emotional state of everyone you interact with

Interestingly stimuli and our reactions are not necessarily displayed like for like in a sensory context.

For instance we may well cover our ears in order not to hear something unpleasant but we are just as likely to close our eyes tightly in order to block out and avoid hearing bad news.

Have you ever seen someone shut their eyes down tightly and proclaim 'don't tell me I don't want to hear even putting their hands up as a barrier to the news. This can be linked to the way the person processes information as discussed next.

Internal language

Another way you can help to build rapport and communicate effectively is to be able to speak the same language as the subject. By this I do not mean the same dialect. Instead speak to them in a way they understand.

If you have read any of my other books you will know about visual accessing cues, and left right brain theory. For those that haven't they are described below. The eyes show us how a person processes information, these cues are very accurate.

The right side of the brain is the creative side of the brain and the left side is the logical side where memories are also kept.

If we ask a person a question and they look right they are trying to imagine something. If they look to their left then they are recalling.

As well as this left right cue we need to know that people think in three different ways too.

Visually   Auditory   Kinesthetically

Visual thinkers tend to look upwards when they are pondering. Auditory types keep their eyes level and those that look down think in terms of feelings and emotions.

So if you were to have conversation with a visual type of person they might use terms like 'oh yes I can see what you are saying' obviously he cannot actually see what you are saying its how he thinks.

An auditory person could say things like 'I hear where you are coming from'.

Finally the kinetic type, these people are tactile and emotional thinkers they use terms such as 'I'd like to get a handle on the situation'.

When dealing with the various types use the language that bests suits them and you will get along a whole lot better.

Putting the eye accessing cues together looks like this By the way the direction indicated it from the subject's point of view

Looking up and to their right
This indicates the subject is trying to imagine in his mind's eye an image.

Looking up and to the left
Again accessing the mind's eye but this time to recall memories.

Looking right
Means they are trying to conjure up sounds in their minds

Looking left
They are recalling or trying to recall sounds.

Down and to the right

Is an attempt to imagine a an emotion or physical feeling

Down and left

Remembering an emotion or physical state.

These eye accessing cues are for right handed people however left handed people may not exclusively use this cue in reverse. Some left hander's also look right to imagine and left to recall.

Comfort zone

Our personal space is very important to us. Proximity of others along with the relationship we have with them has a bearing on our responses.

For instance if your spouse stands within a few inches of you, this is quite natural and there would be no problem, your body language would remain relaxed or neutral.

If however a total stranger were to stand this close the responses would be vastly different.

In the field of psychology it is generally accepted that there are four spaces in which we interact with others. These spaces are known as communication zones.

1/ The Public space

2/ Social Space

3/ Personal Space

4/ Intimate space

Public.

This space is anything further than twelve feet (3.6 metres) away from us. At this distance we are not really interacting with anyone on a personal level. If we spotted someone that we did want to talk to we would have to get their attention and move toward them. Conversely we could just as easily avoid them completely.

From the point of view of survival and our instinctive response, if danger presented itself at this distance we would almost certainly freeze whilst gauging the level of threat or until the danger had passed.

Social space.

From our original twelve, feet right down to four feet (3.6 metres to 1.2 metres). This is the area in which normal social activities take place a gathering at a dinner party or a group of friends having a good time at a pub. Communicating can be anything from cordial exchanges to friendly conversation.

Looking at this from the survival point of view. If danger presented itself in this area we would certainly freeze and probably be considering our two options flight or fight.

Personal space

This is from about four feet right down to a very close eighteen inches (1.2 metres to 45 centimetres), away from us.

This area is reserved for friends, and other trusted individuals in this area we would be interacting and perhaps having some form of physical contact such as shoulder touching.

An exception to this would be during an introduction when say a handshake is appropriate. The general environment would be deemed safe or the handshake could not take place.

Survival: if a danger presented itself in this personal space area then flight would definitely occur even if running were a futile act. Our limbic brain simply would not allow any other response. If our ancestors came across a predator at these distances he would, if he had time, run in the opposite direction without fail. Of course because of the initial freeze this distance may have meant disaster anyway.

Intimate space

This area is reserved for spouses, family and close friends. At this distance, anywhere closer than eighteen inches, interactions are as the title implies intimate. Here is for hugging kissing and the like.

Survival in this particular area is last ditch stuff. So as you can see our imaginary ancestor coming across danger at this distance would have no option but to fight since he has already been cornered.

Interestingly there are exceptions to this too. That exception is the 'crowd'

If we are on a crowded train, elevator or when in a theatre.

We are forced into each other's intimate space. Here social niceties take precedence.

Under these circumstances we make kind open gestures and sounds to each other, we are temporarily accepting that invasion of this space is necessary for the greater good and that it is only temporary.

The purpose of the politeness is to show that we will not be a threat and to disarm the other person or persons.

One of the places where it is amusing to watch the intimate 'space invasion' is in a queue. Here the individuals are mindful not to encroach whilst at the same time not wanting to be seen as too far back and not in line.

The facial expressions in queues alone would make for a very entertaining study. Next time you see a queue watch peoples expressions of worry and their observations of others.

It is worth remembering this relationship between comfort zones and the fright to fight responses. As you can see proximity will affect the reactions and the level of those reactions very much.

Another point which must be taken into account is that not only does closeness cause greater response also that our own behaviour can and will affect the response of those we are trying to read.

If we are a bit too intense in our observation the subject will sense this and their non verbal signals will change as part of their defense mechanisms.

It will also lead to incongruence especially if they are feeling uncomfortable.

Always be as neutral as possible.

One of the things parents learn to do is to be neutral and even handed with their children. If they weren't they would never hear the truth.

Aggressive questioning or observation will cause discomfort no matter what and will also create non cooperation by the subject either consciously or unconsciously.

Tells

This is the buzz word used in non verbal circles to describe the reaction being read by the observer. What is the person telling us with his body language or other non verbal communications?

We also call them reads it's the same thing in reverse instead of being told what the message is we are reading the message. So throughout the book when I refer to tells and reads they are effectively the same thing from a different perspective.

Reading

Firstly there is a stimulus or input. This can come in the form of a question, a statement, a sight a sound anything really.

Then there is the reaction on the part of the subject. The reaction is where it gets interesting because they come in so many forms and all have different meanings as we will see throughout this book. This initial reaction will be in the form of a micro expression or micro movement. Or an intention reaction or cue.

Thirdly one of two things will happen either the micro expression continues into a full expression or movement or posture or the conscious takes over and covers the micro (true) expression with one which the subject wishes to project. The masking.

The last thing to occur especially if the stimulus is seen as unsavoury will be the comforter.

And we are back into the realms of instinct again. Comforters again happen in real time unconsciously and often, as with micro expressions, they can be gone in a second if the conscious becomes aware of the movement and masks it.

Sometimes one more thing happens. If the person has got away with it or they think they have they will poke their tongue out at you. Quite literally again this will be a micro tongue jut but it will be there.

Practice

There is only one way to polish up those skills and become an expert body language reader and that is to practise. Start practising as soon as you have read the book. Study people in the street in coffee shops in bars absolutely everywhere. Look first for very overt things. Things that are easy to see.

Watching pairs of people talking and seeing their comfort levels through their bodies is not too hard because you can look at the whole picture. Don't go straight from the book to interrogating your family and friends.

Another excellent way to practice is to watch one of the so called relationship shows on TV. The type where they have DNA paternity tests and lie detector tests to catch cheating spouses etc.

Only watch it with the sound down and make some notes as to what you think the people on stage are feeling. Then watch it with the sound up and you may be surprised that you have correctly predicted the general emotions being displayed.

Ask friends to help you. Get them to answer half a dozen questions for you. Tell them to answer correctly five times and to lie once. Make sure it is not something you already know the answer to. Do this over and over and eventually you will begin to see the little giveaways.

If you are trying to determine micro expressions one on one then you need to take a snapshot as you deliver the stimuli and refer back to what you saw. The problem is that the expression lasts such a short amount of time you get sucked into reading a bigger timeframe. So snapshot at the reaction and even look away if you need to.

Also if you want to see how true they are simply go to a full length mirror and mimic the poses and expressions described in the book and you will see for yourself they are an accurate guide.

Keep in mind all the above when making reads. You must know what the person is usually like under normal conditions.

Baseline

Although there are a lot of universal signals which are easily read when watching people interact socially. Whenever reading non verbal's on an individual or one to one basis it is essential to establish a baseline, that is to say what the general demeanour of the individual is and how they behave under normal neutral conditions.

For instance you have probably heard before now that when you come across someone with their arms crossed in front of them, that this automatically means they are closed off, unreceptive or even angry, under some circumstances this may be true, but there are also some people out there for whom this is a comfortable normal posture.

This brings us to the need to have a start point of how n individual behaves under 'normal' conditions.

We need to identify their little idiosyncrasies and for that matter there more obvious oddities. Many people have twitches and movements which they make habitually and without identifying these you may be lead up the garden path, especially if these idiosyncrasies could easily fall into one of the universal indicators categories we discuss later.

We Need to determine personality types, some are nervy types and can give off non verbal messages that something is wrong some may be so laid back they'd almost falling over backwards.

The trick is to look for all these things and once you have that baseline of behaviour look for change in the non verbal to individual stimuli also one thing alone is not always reliable it is better to have multiple indicators in order to make sure you are reading the signals being sent out correctly.

You need to see normal (for the individual) reactions to normal inputs in order to establish a reliable baseline.

For example the aforementioned arms crossed as a comfortable neutral position for some people. What might be telling, is if the person unfolds their arms and in reaction to what has been said to them or something they have seen etc.

Comforters

One more thing to mention is the soothers or comforters. These are nerve ending stimulators designed to create comfort.

When a comforter follows a reaction that is a sure sign of discomfort. Soothers come in all shapes and sizes.

As I said it is the process of stimulating nerve endings, it sends a message to the brain that says 'there there 'everything will be just fine' so rubbing just about any part of the body hand to hand, hand to a shoulders hand to leg is a sign that a person is comforting themselves. The question is of course why?

One of the universal comforters, when I say universal I mean that just about every sane person on the planet does it, is the puffing of the cheeks and blowing out air between pursed lips after a close call or an emotionally charged event. It's the 'phew' effect.

Another universal comforter is self hugging, this is a replication of the safe feelings given to us by our parents, reassurance hugs, joyous hugs and hug's just to show general love and affection. We self hug and touch In order to feel safe and secure.

For proof that body language is natural and instinctive behaviour we can turn to the animal kingdom, because animals have no guile. When it comes to being in danger they truly do rely upon and react to their 'animal instincts'

Any animal which is not a natural predator when startled will first freeze and assess the danger like a deer in the headlights of a car.

Next it will turn and run to gain as much distance as possible

If is finally cornered it will turn and fight.

As for comforting itself watch your own adult pets. They lick themselves, yes of course this is part of the grooming and cleaning routine but also this is a feel safe process.

They are in fact replicating the mothers licking when it was young which makes them feel safe.

Particularly watch them when they are unwell, regardless of the cause of their state they will lick themselves constantly

Universal changes.

In my other books on hypnosis you will read that a change in the emotional state changes the physical body and vice versa. So what happens in the head and heart affects the body.

We have looked at the universal behaviours now it's time to look at universal changes in behaviour which signify not only whether the emotional state of the subject has changed in either a positive or negative manner but also to what degree that emotional change has occurred.

So when you see the subject go from one of the states below to another you know there has been a change

Up is good

Confident, content or comfortable. The higher up the happier we are, the better we are feeling regardless of the individual situation. This relates to hands arms feet head shoulders and even our whole body.

Levitation gestures of any sort are psychological thumbs up having said that even the thumbs up are a positive sign.

Down is bad

Lack of confidence, low self esteem, fear, discomfort. The unhappier we are the lower we go. Again you will see that the worse we feel the more we shrink down and attempt minimise our bodily footprint.

Width

Is confidence, arrogance, disdain, the more alpha male we are being the wider we go. Not just our body in this instance. Taking space can be done using objects like paperwork etc at a business meeting.

Large movements

Are confident movements when a person is confident and talking they will use their hands and whole body sometimes to emphasise

Small movements

Show low confidence. When someone is not confident their movement is generally small even robotic at times.

It has been said that liars do not use large expressive movements. This may or may not be true. Remember the above mantra.

Establish your baseline then look for change when stimuli is received. If there is a marked change then the stimuli affected the person's emotional state.

Watch people at a football game when their team is behind and it's getting late on in the game. Thousands of people puffing their cheeks, rubbing their legs, wringing their hands they have crumpled faces as if in physical pain.

Then their team scores and avoids defeat. They jump up their arms go up they stamp their feet and cheer. They are not copying one another these are universal non verbal communication signals, Handed down by our ancestors. This is tribal stuff and we are all prone.

Preening

Before we go on I should mention preening or grooming. This is the act of titivating oneself in an attempt to show ourselves off in a good light. Making sure we look our best and are as attractive as possible to the opposite sex.

The Top

HEAD

Head touching

Touching of the head and hair is very significant behaviour and the messages depend on the type of touching that is done.

Comfort

An obvious one for both men and women is the running of the fingers through their hair. This is an overt form of grooming. It is often done in front of someone we are attracted to.

It is saying look not only should you notice me but I am clean, I groom myself and I am healthy pick me!

Women will also flick their hair by quickly rotating the head from their chin upwards and backwards this behaviour is overtly flirtatious. It says look at me!

Discomfort

Pushing our fingers and hands through our hair in slow deliberate movements is also done at times of high stress.

We even go as far as clasping our head when we are highly uncomfortable. Both hands go up to the sides of our head and our fingers spread as wide as possible. It's almost as if we are forming a motorcycle crash helmet around it in order to protect it from uncomfortable information.

Some people play with their hair; this can be put down to habit but is also identifiable as a comforter

When you see someone with both hands on the top of their head with the head tilted forward this is a comforter. It can be a quick motion say out our infamous football game when his team missed a shot. It can be prolonged.

If it is prolonged it can often be the regretful thought position. This position can be held for quite some time while the person reflects internally over some mishap. Often the person is saying to themselves 'why me' or 'if only I had...'

When rubbing the hair and head in firm repeated backward strokes this is a definite comforter. Lighting up those all important nerve endings in both the palms and the head. This gesture is more common in men that women. Probably stems from male to male bonding, when a father approves or is playful with their sons they often rub their heads as a show of affection rather than hugging.

Head scratching can sometimes indicate conflict or confusion. We often hear of a difficult problem as being 'a real head scratcher'. Accompanied by facial expressions of thought or confusion.

Subjects often play with their hair as an aid to thinking. Literally touching the point on the body which is doing the work almost like trying to gently pull the thoughts out.

Head Nodding

Nodding in western cultures is a universal sign of agreement.

The faster the nod the more in agreement they are.

A very slow no can mean that third is mutual respect but not necessarily full agreement.

Head nod down in deference if this is the intention then the upper torso will tend to lean at the same time. You can see this movement in the presence of heads of states and the like. Depending on the importance of the person and the protocols this head nod may turn into a full torso bow.

Head nod down in brief acknowledgement you see this between business men where the space between them does not allow for interaction at a personal space distance.

Head nod up in acknowledgement similar to the above. Obviously the head is moving up instead of down and it is reserved for less formal acquaintances and friends.

Head nod in approval or encouragement. Can be any speed depending on the circumstances. The facial expression must be read as well.

Head Shake

Shaking of the head is the opposite of the head nod and of course it indicates a negative response.

The faster the shake the more in disagreement the subject is.

A very slow shake can mean there is a feeling of disdain

The Freudian (head) slip

Is when a person is saying one thing and the instinctive brain is replying in the exact opposite. A good example is if you are making a statement to someone and they are denying whatever it is you say but all the time the head is going up and down unconsciously you can be almost certain that the head is telling the truth.

The opposite is when we do the Freudian no head slip. Someone is telling you something which you think is untrue or that you at least disagree with. Whilst politely agreeing your head moves almost imperceptibly left and right signifying that you are merely waiting for them to finish before telling them 'not a chance'. This can be construed as impolite by the reader since it is obvious there is no intention of compliance. You've already cut them off and are not really listening

A word here if you are trying to detect an untruth look for multiple displays as well as comforters some people simply nod their heads when being addressed to confirm they are assimilating the information.

In some eastern cultures the head nod and shake are reversed. A shaking head is used for emphasis and agreement.

Head up

Is generally a sign of confidence? This confidence can often go one step further though.

If the head is held too high so that the subject is looking down their nose at you then they are showing superiority.

When the head is held up this high and the eyes sort of over relax slightly then this is a definite show of arrogance.

Although head tilting is dealt with in more detail in the neck section it is interesting to know that Women tilt their head as a sign of interest and or flirtation.

Head down

This is a classic sign of low confidence, it is a prime example of 'down is bad'.

The head drop is a sign of universal discomfort often seen in defeat along with neck rubbing comforters.

If the head is down and the eyes still looks up at another person or objects beware this could be the look of contempt or even hatred.

A drooping head along with slack expression is an overt show of boredom. It is considered very rude to overtly allow this expression to be displayed in social or professional environments.

Head flick

A very slight movement of the head up in an almost unnoticeable flick is a sign that the subject does not believe he is hearing the truth. The instinctive system is attempting to dismiss the information and the giver of it. It is the head movement equivalent of shooing away with the hand.

Be careful not to misread this as a micro head nod which goes down very slightly.

Face

The face can lie and very often does, we are taught from a very early age to deceive. In order to save others feeling is one of the reason, although I believe 'the truth will set you free'.

When we tell these white lies and are encouraged by adults to do so we quickly become very good at it. So we learn to tell an untruth and keep a perfectly normal looking set of expressions, we can even go so far as to fake expressions, just like when we have prior knowledge of an event and we have a complete look of surprise on our face when we are told about it.

Even this 'false face' though is a mask. And masking does not appear in real time.

Remember that micro expression is the indicator of true emotion and these are uncensored. They also happen in real time as the stimuli is received.

It is therefore critically important to learn as much as you can about facial expression then practise the art of identifying them as they appear in micro-expressions .

On the opposite side of the coin when we use false expression we sometimes tend to hold the 'look' for too long in an attempt to force home the non verbal communication. Another common side effect is over-exaggerating the expression. So watch out for everything.

Although you should be watching for everything be very careful.

Social convention must be observed when reading body language and especially the face.

Only hold the subjects gaze for what would be socially acceptable. If you look longer than would be normal the subject will become uncomfortable, once they become uncomfortable their whole demeanour will change and the reading process will be impossible due to overt signals. Especially true if they have taken offence.

The neutral look for most is a generally relaxed facial expression. Skin colour will vary greatly with changes in the environment and mood.

Skin showing a healthy colour in average heat conditions may appear reddened in hotter weather and paler than usual in the cold.

Mood also affects the colour in the face reddening of the face can indicate anything from anger to embarrassment, pallid skin is usually associated with discomfort, the blood drains when we are shocked

As I have mentioned and will continue to do so multiple reads must be observed.

Any contortion of the face is out of the norm generally speaking. Contortion can indicate anything from physical pain to mental or emotional discomfort. Of course there is also the fact that our face contorts to smile and laugh.

Touching of the hands to the face is one of the most common activities us humans do, we touch our face over a hundred times a day.

Although we do this for a multitude of reasons the overall purpose is to reassure. The lightest of finger touches when browsing in a shop to resting our face in our hands after a tiring day at the shops. Face touching can mean everything or nothing.

There are 44 muscles in the face allowing an almost infinite variation of expressions depending on how they are flexed.

Forehead

The forehead is highly visible at all times and is often ignored, which is a mistake since it is a good overall indicator of mood. Changes in the skin of the forehead usually accompany expression changes.

Forehead rubbing is associated with thinking as if we can physically massage the information out

Pushing the fingers or the palm of the hand to the forehead is a sign that the person could either be recalling something which is usually accompanied by statements such as 'it's on the tip of my tongue' or 'give me a moment'. In this case the head usually stays level although tilting the head up or down is not uncommon.

Pushing the fingers against the forehead can also indicate an 'oh no' moment' then, unlike when attempting to recall information, the head usually drops forward into the fingers or hand and can even shake from side to side sometimes almost imperceptibly, a sign of internal discomfort. Of course this is the universal no signal or in this case more likely the 'OH NO' signal

The same also goes for placing the fingers to the temple area. It can be a physical attempt to help the memory cogs go around or the 'oh no' moment. Again look for the head staying steady or facing up or going forward and down. Remember up is good down is not.

Also people tend to put their fingers to their temples if they are feeling overwhelmed. Although the pose is exactly the same as trying to remember it can also be to try and slow down the rate of stimuli.

Allow for the fact that someone may simply have a headache and is massaging their temples. Just remember that a headache is uncomfortable which simply helps to prove that rubbing the forehead is a comforter.

The furrowed brow this is when we push our eyebrows down slightly creating a stern look the vertical lines on our forehead become more pronounced.

The surprise, shock or fear furrow is horizontally rather than vertical.

Eyebrows

From the non verbal perspective the eyebrows connect the forehead to the eyes. So they will move in accordance with either or both of them.

Another is that they are very prone to micro movements because we become aware of the movement of them very easily and so mask them almost the second they appear.

When practicing, looking for subtle clues to the genuine emotional state, start with the eyebrows.

One eyebrow raised is a look of questioning. They have had some input and are asking for more information often seen with the hand, palm up moving slightly toward the other person.

If the eyes are widened at the same time accompanied by a smile then you are witnessing an intimate interest usually this signaling is reserved for romantic partners. As a micro expression it shows interest but also that the subject is not willing to show this interest. A good example would be when two parties are bargaining.

When both eyebrows flinch up wards at the same time again as a micro expression the person is surprised by what they are seeing or hearing

If the eyebrows move upwards more slowly and deliberately then the information being received is truthful the brain is experiencing a mild form of conflict.

Eyebrows which move towards the middle of the face in a squinting motion are showing concern.

When the head is tilted forward and the subject is looking at you from under their eyebrows they are openly signifying dominance and defiance.

When the eyebrows fly up this is a sign of recognition. When this is held and is accompanied by positive facial expression it is happy surprise. If it is a flash in the pan this is not so good.

Another 'flash' of the eyebrows is a sure sign of recognition this can be anything from seeing a person to internally confirming a particular stimuli. For instance when being accused of an act instead of showing surprise they show recognition. This person may be guilty!

Inside of the eyebrow raises along with wide eyes is a clear expression of surprise. Sometimes this eyebrow movement is accompanied by a sharp intake of breath when this happens it is more likely to be shock or fear rather than surprise

Eyebrows that go down at the innermost point accompanied by narrowing of the eyes are n overt expression of anger. If you see this as a micro expression which is then masked beware.

When the inner eyebrow rises up and the sides of the face condense inwards this means the person is either experiencing sadness or is empathising with someone

Eyes

Before looking at the eyes and all they can tell us remember to use the eye accessing cue guideline. The full explanation is in chapter one but I will repeat the overview in the interests of not having to go back and forth. The direction of the eyes below is from the subjects point of view up and right is to their right. And to your left

Up and right visually imagining

Up and left visually recalling

Right accessing audio imagination

Left accessing audio memory

Down and right imagining emotions or physical feeling.

Down and left remembering emotions or physical feelings.

Eyes it is said are the windows to the soul, well from the instinctive brain point of view they are certainly a window into the mind.

Given this window idea we can easily understand why we do some of the things we do. From opening wide when things are good to let the images in and savour the moment. To closing them when things are not good as if to not see something means it can't affect them.

Eye Blocking

Blocking of the eyes is done is an attempt to protect the brain from seeing something distressing this includes closing the eyelids or squinting right up to putting a hand or forearm up in front of them.

When blocking of the eyes is accompanied by a forward tilt of the head it can indicate that the person does not believe or disagrees with what is being put to them. This behaviour can also occur in a person who is struggling with a piece of information or is thinking intensely.

Eye touching is borderline micro gesture it happens very briefly and is a blocking gesture. It can be as brief as a light stroking of the eyebrow to leaving a finger resting on the outer edges of the eye lid.

Keeping the eyes closed for a lengthy period, or what might seem an unnaturally long time is an eye block to shut out interference while we contemplate.

Usually it indicates a conflict or struggle between opposing ideas. Such as when you confront a child and they know that the 'it was like that when I found it' line will no longer work. It is as if they are hiding the eyes as they come to terms with the change of heart.

Compressing the lids down is a blocking gesture which actually makes the face look as if it is in pain. Watch someone receiving bad news such as being unsuccessful in gaining a contract. The eyelids compress down. This is also done in conjunction with a shaking of the head as if refusing to hear or see the evidence of bad news.

Blinking of the eyelids can occur in the full range of emotion from deep joy to complete fear. Watch for a change in the blinking rate from baseline.

Interestingly we also do block our eyes to shut out audio information. When someone either receives or is expecting to hear bad news we often display some of the above actions.

Pupils

Dilated pupils. Most of us associate this with drug taking thanks to popular press etc. Dilation happens when we are relaxed and comfortable. Watch two young people in love gazing into each other's eyes and you will see their pupils are dilated. Dilated pupils show interest

Partial dilation. This is a sign of scepticism the subject is not yet on board but has not completely lost interest.

Constricted pupils are a form of biological blocking of input into the eyes. The subject has lost interest completely. Often accompanied by a glazed over or faraway look. Sometimes it appears they are looking right through you. It is the look of a hypnotized person.

Looking for clues in the pupils of the eyes is obviously very difficult since we have to be very close to the subject and there is no way you can disguise the fact that you are looking at the subject.

Other eye movement

Eye wonderment. This is the big wow eyes we make when we are pleasantly surprised or amazed this is a high comfort gesture.

Looking sideways whilst keeping our head facing forward is a distrustful look. This one is sometimes done not as the result of direct input but rather as a reaction to the person themselves. I have witnessed this eye movement in a subject even when the object of their distrust is not present. When talking about a distrusted person the subject looked sideways as he said 'I wouldn't believe a word he says'

Rolling eyes up is a disrespectful gesture and when it is done it is impossible not to see it.

Nose

The nose is often completely overlooked, this is a mistake.

The nose is interesting because it takes a lot of effort to use the muscles associated with it.

This means that as soon as it is not just sitting there in a neutral pose the subject notices it. Therefore it is a good source for micro expression. There is a common expression 'follow your nose' well this has some foundation. Have you ever seen the magic trick where the magician guesses which hand his victim has an object in? I'll assume you have.

Well the reason the magician is always right is because he is able to read micro movements. Even when the victim has their eyes pointed forward the nose will turn very slightly toward the hand that he has the object in.

Crinkling of the nose is.

This is when the nose is pulled up and horizontal lines appear on the bridge right between the eyes is often accompanied by a furrowing of the brow. The person displaying this behaviour looks like they smell a bad smell. This isn't far from the truth because to the instinctive brain seeing hearing or smelling something which disgusts us will cause us to crinkle our nose.

So a nose crinkle is a sign of disgust or distaste. There are variations on the crinkle for instance sometimes it will only happen to one side, and often it is in unison with a sneer. This is also a very common micro expression which is quickly covered with a polite false smile.

Nose flare.

Flaring nostrils is a bad sign. It literally happens in order to open the nostrils more than usual to allow more oxygen to be taken in, nearly always you will notice either a sharp intake of breath or a deeper than usual breathe, another thing is that the person will tend to 'plant' their feet. These are all signs that the person has reached the fight response. Of course this may not mean that things are about to get physical. It is definitely a sign that the person is determined to stand their ground whether it is in negotiation or an argument.

So if the nostrils flare be aware if you are the subject of the response take a step back

The nostrils also flare when we are becoming aroused. So as always look for the signs in groups of behaviour and of course in context.

High nose

A nose held high is a sign of aloofness; this has a natural tendency of making the person look down, hence the expression 'look down your nose'.

Interestingly when less tall people want to demonstrate this aloofness they sometimes have to tilt their heads back quite a way to do so, making it even more pronounces.

Seeing someone shorter than yourself doing this can look quite unnatural and even comical. Watch out for this one you will love it when you see it. It can appear they are actually talking to the ceiling.

As a footnote to the last passage tall people often stoop in order to avoid projecting this air of authority.

Cheeks

Touching of the cheek with the fingers is done for many reasons of course some people do this from pure habit

Many people do this when they are daydreaming or when they thinking it sometimes moves on from just touching the cheek to chin cupping and even back to cheek touching. When this happens you are witnessing a fluctuation in the intensity of the thoughts.

Resting the cheek on an open fist is a variation of the thinker pose.

Of course there are plenty of nerve endings in the cheeks and so touching the cheeks is also a very effective comforter.

Puffing cheeks

Puffing up of the cheeks and then letting the air out through pursed lips is a very intense comforter. This is a universal comforter and we do it whenever we have avoided something uncomfortable or something uncomfortable has happened and it is finally over.

Cheek colour

Cheek colour can also be very significant

Reddening or blushing, the cheeks become flushed with blood and the face becomes hotter.

This is an emotional reaction universal to all of us. However the actual emotion being displayed can range from embarrassment right through to rage.

There are other physical reasons of the cheeks to redden and this may be actual ambient temperature. The general heat that a person is experience can easily give a false positive of an emotional reaction.

Cheek biting

Biting the inside of the cheek is a sign of discomfort. Often this cheek biting will cause some very severe movement of the entire face with the person not even realising how contorted they look. Gently bite the inside of your cheek whilst looking in the mirror, it's quite comical.

Lips

Pursed lips are when we make the lips small round and tight. We do this when we are displeased.

The level of displeasure of course has to be taken into consideration. A parent pursing their lips along with their eyebrows raised may be indicating that they are not pleased with a school report or theirs Childs behaviour. Someone displaying pursed lips and a furrowed brow along with flared nostrils may have reached the end of their tether and become very angry, this is more like the pursed lips of the headmaster just about to expel the aforementioned child from school.

Pursed lips may also indicate disagreement with what is being heard or seen.

Disappearing lips

When the lips are compressed and turn inwards almost disappearing from view altogether the sign is that they are physically stopping something coming out of their mouths, when as the expression goes 'holding our tongue'.

They have something to say but choose not to say it. You may see this during a conversation whilst one person is talking the one listening does this lip disappearing.

When their time comes they will almost always have something negative to say about what it is they heard.

Another display of disappearing lips may occur when a person simply has something to say but has decided not to.

This is not a guaranteed signal for lying. It may be that the subject simply has a secret. The lips are literally showing you 'my lips are sealed' but if you see this behaviour in response to a question look for further clues such as comforting actions and other signs of discomfort.

Sometimes we see pursed lips from those who have been sidelined in a multi person exchange. Often in committee or board meetings, if this happens you could do the polite thing and ask if they have something on their mind, you never know they could have something very important to say.

Lip licking

Licking of the lips is a universal comforting behaviour. Of course their lips could always be dry especially in winter. But dryness also occurs when we are under stress

Rubbing the lips from side to side with our tongue is a sign of discomfort and of contemplation.

Biting lips

There are many reasons a person may bite their lips and the messages are vastly different as you will see below, I am going to mention this one last time remember to look for multiple tells, consider the situation and context as well as compare to baseline.

We see people biting their lips when they are anxious. It is similar to cheek biting and is a universal comforter.

Biting lips as a flirting gesture girls do this in order to look coy and vulnerable which makes them attractive to men.

Lip biting shows is also a Tell that someone is feeling empathy for another. It is seen when an individual witnesses another in pain or distress

Lip biting may be substituted and augmented by using a prop such as a pencil. In this case it is being used as a comforter. Using cigarettes has the same effect.

Stiff lips

Stiff upper lip we have this expression in the UK. It is not only an expression but it is a physical act.

It is a means of staving off emotion in an attempt to underpin our resolve. It is nearly impossible to allow your face to show sadness with a stiff upper lip.

Pouting.

Pouting occurs for differing reasons. and should be read in context to determine the correct signal. OK that's really the last time I mention it.

Pouting with furrowed brow will mean displeasure or sadness

Pouting with slightly widened eyes to show interest

Pouting with a glazes distant look in the eyes happens when we are deep in thought

Tongue

Obviously a very delicate part of the anatomy it is also very sensitive. You could be mistaken for thinking that it has little to do with body language since is hidden away inside the mouth. This couldn't be further from the truth.

Winning tongue

Watch children at play in a game that is competitive in some way, football, cops 'n' robbers or cowboys and Indians, you will often see that when one child is victorious over the other in one of these games the winner will poke their tongue out letting the other know they have had one over on them.

They are saying you 'I am better than you'. Of course with young children this is not malicious it only means he is better in this particular game.

Losing Tongue

Interestingly the loser will often poke their tongue back at the winner. In this case it is a gesture of defiance and distain. The loser is saying 'I don't care it's not important to me'.

Not caring tongue

Another version of this tongue poking by children is when they get caught out doing something. They will turn and poke their tongue about and say 'so what'

Got away with tongue

Finally the tongue comes out as if to say you didn't catch me.

Concentrating tongue

Poking our tongue out is a very significant behaviour. We are showing that we are so moved that we are willing to expose a very important part of our body which is usually kept safe and sound.

Often adults will overtly poke their tongues out at one another. If it is overt then it is in jest to mock their own self by acknowledging their childish behaviour.

Now when we look at the more subtle adult version of this tongue poke, a jutting tongue, it should set alarm bells ringing.

This is seen when the tongue protrudes between the lips which are kept closed, it appears that the tongue is forcing its way forward and it generally only comes out by a millimetre or two

It often very appears as a micro expression but it is there nonetheless. This tongue jut is no different meaning than the previous childish actions.

It appears as a micro expression when someone thinks they have won or more accurately, has got away with something

Just like our defeated child it also shows disgust.

Some people when using this expression can't help themselves and display a micro smile at the same time a. if you notice these two things together its almost certain you've been had and probably in no small way.

Rubbing the tongue along the front of the teeth with the mouth closed is an act of confidence it's a modified preening display.

Mouth

This is an interesting part of the anatomy when it comes to reading non verbals, mostly because it is the source of the verbal. It also is capable of whispering, shouting, screaming, singing and even kissing.

Because we are taught from an early age to lie, either to save the feelings of others or to get away with something our mouth is quite adept at it and along with the trained responses we use to control our expression we are often successful.

What is interesting is what happens to our mouth before during and after we lie. In essence don't necessarily believe all you are told but do believe the micro intention clues and the comforters.

Whistling

In some places around the globe this is a very offensive habit. Some cultures feel it encroaches upon them even though there is no physical act of entering the comfort zones.

Sometimes when people whistle it is a sign of nervousness and discomfort but sometimes it is just habit.

If it is habit then how did it become a habit? Interestingly the habit was formed because of nervousness. Initially the subject would have whistled when nervous say having to walk down a dark alley or something similar.

After whistling enough times and feeling the benefit of the comforter it becomes used so often the unconscious takes it on as a habit. If you look at most habits that mimic comforters then the same follows for them as for whistling. If you want to know more about how habits are formed then read my other books on hypnosis.

Yawn

Yawning can indicate discomfort. If you ask someone a question and they do an excessively long yawn before or even during the reply this shows that they were uncomfortable about what was coming out of their mouth. It serves two purposes. It squints the eyes slightly in an attempt to eye block and operates as a comforter because of all the nerves it activates as the mouth stretches.. If you see someone does this in answer to a question be alert.

Don't forget people yawn when they are tired, also yawning is as infectious as a smile, once one person starts the rest usually follow. You should be able to spot a natural yawn with very little practice.

Smile

A genuine smile makes the cheeks rise up and out towards the ears, dimples appear at the corners of the mouth, and the eyes also soften with the corners crinkled. Along with these facial signs the head will often tilt slightly to one side. Anything other than this is a false smile.

False smile

The lips stretch across the face horizontally and there is no corresponding emotional content visible in the eyes. Sometimes the outside of the lips actually curve downwards slightly.

There is a variation of the false smile; this is the overtly big smile. The pantomime smile the mouth goes up as with a genuine smile the eyes also crinkle but they do not soften as a result. This is the condescending false smile. When you see the condescending false smile the person has no respect for you.

Upside down smile

Very low confidence also seen during weeping.

As with all downward motions a sign of distress of one kind or another. The upside down smile can sometimes be seen along with disappearing lips.

It almost looks like the person getting away with something feels compassion toward their victim.

The sneer.

This is a one sided smile almost exclusively seen as a micro expression, this look shows complete disrespect for the person to which it is directed.

Agog

The mouth wide open can be in complete awe. Often seen at an event for instance a fireworks display the crowd will let out a 'wow' and then the mouth stays open because they are so engrossed in what they are watching.

Another wide open mouth often occurs during daydreaming when the person sort of over relaxes. My grandmother would call this the 'catching flies' expression and say a 'penny for your thoughts'

The grin.

The grin can just be subdued versions of a smile or a false smile.

Sometimes it is a sort of two sided sneer, if it is it will be accompanied with a nose crinkle.

Chin

Another saying I trust you've all heard. 'Chin up!' It's what we say to people when they are down in the doldrums as if by lifting their chin will magically lift their mood.

Well it's not actually that ridiculous. As with all other body language Tells up is good. Down is bad.

So lifting the chin or even 'pulling your socks up, is a physical manifestation of digging in deep and rising up to meet whatever challenge has to be met.

When the chin is level or even slightly up this is a show of confidence. This is where we get the expression 'chin up' from.

If it goes up quite a way it can signify they are attempting to look down their nose at you. (See section on noses).

Chin down means confidence is also down. This literally requires the head to be tilted forward. The closer the chin drops toward the chest the lower the confidence.

Watch a child being berated by a parent the longer it goes on the lower the chin goes.

It is also a great eye blocker. That is why at the end of the telling off the parent will tell the child to look up? It is in order to confirm the message has been understood.

It is also a universal comforter since we drop it in attempt to cover the neck dimple. See next section.

Chin (or jaw drop) can show amazement and disbelief. This is an expression seldom misread. Even in its micro form because of the whole of the bottom jaw dropping and coming back up takes so long compared to most micro expressions which only last about a tenth of a second it is reasonably easily noticeable

Locked jaw

Whether the mouth is open or closed is a good indicator of stress. This lock can sometimes be held for a very long time, in fact the longer it is held the more tension there is. Look for other reads for clues as to what else is going on.

Neck

The neck is a very delicate area of the body and in times of danger or worry we feel a need to protect it. Conversely when we are comfortable we don't mind having it exposed. The more we expose the more comfortable we are.

To the front is the beck dimple, this is the hollow at the top of the breastbone, in men it is below the Adams apple. This is a very vulnerable part of the anatomy.

To the left and right of this dimple almost on the sides the carotid arteries link the head to the body. These again are very vulnerable areas.

If ever you watch a television documentary about predators in the wild watch which part of the prey's body they aim for. It is nearly always the neck once a lion has its jaw and teeth around its victim's throat it is all over

Neck exposure

Laying the head over to the side exposes these areas so this is a high comfort indicator allowing access even if only visually to this area is not only showing but also inviting trust.

When this neck exposure is engaged in it is important to remember the left and right brain theory.

If you expose your left side that is to say your head has tilted to the right then you are communicating emotionally with your cohort.

If however the right side is exposed by left head tilting then the logical side of the brain is being used. Watch out for this it's really fun to watch and accurate.

Two business men talking about a project may tilt their heads to the left exposing their right neck in acceptance of a theory. While romantic partners or people flirting will expose their left side of the neck

Covering the neck dimple,

Any touching or covering of the neck is a negative non verbal sign no matter how fleeting. A single touch with a single finger can be just as telling as a full palm pressed against the neck.

It is a universal comforter It can be anything from a light touching when we are unsure to completely covering when we experience fear.

This dimple covering does not necessarily mean actually touching with the hand it can take different more subtle movement.

Playing with a necklace for a woman is a form of dimple covering.

Adjusting a tie for a man is part of this comforting behaviour

Tie adjustment can take place as a man prepares for a task it's a quick last check that everything is in place before moving forward. It's a sort of grooming act.

Loosening of the collar is a discomfort sign too. Although it is more likely that it is an attempt to ventilate the neck rather than cover it. You've all heard the expression 'hot under the collar'. Well that is exactly what happens. Discomfort causes heat.

Rubbing a hand around the inside of the collar, often seen with a neck stretch is a similar ventilating comforter.

Touching the sides or back of our neck is also a very powerful comforter and again this is universal to us all. Seeing this behaviour indicates a degree of discomfort. Along with other indicators and in context you can figure out what has caused the discomfort.

Touching the neck just below the chin can be a flirting gesture. Especially if seen with a slight head tilt. When women do this be careful not to confuse Dimple covering. The hand will be closer to the chin than the dimple.

Women may use accessories to achieve this 'come on' gesture for example playing with a necklace and touching it to their neck.

Fuel gauge

Neck covering fuel gauge, if you watch a woman in conversation and her arm is across her or on top of a table this is a good sign she is comfortable.

Her discomfort fuel gauge is nonexistent or empty. If her hand comes up towards her neck she is becoming uncomfortable. The higher the hand the more full the discomfort tank, just like a fuel gauge on a car dashboard.

If someone leans their head to one side whilst telling you something and at the very same time they touch their neck then you have almost certainly just been told an untruth.

It is an attempt to disarm with a submissive head tilt, which under normal circumstances might be accompanied by a smile or other friendly facial expression, coupled with a grand comforter.

The Middle

Shoulders

Because they are such a large part of the anatomy it is actually easy to dismiss them whilst trying to look for micro expressions and small non verbal signals.

Ignore the shoulders at your peril. They are a very good indicator of the general emotional state of an individual.

Note their position when you start your baseline. Since they are often the first part of the body to make a move. They are good backup when attempting multiple reads, if you see a non verbal sign and the shoulders confirm your direction of thought coupled with a comforter you can be pretty sure your conclusion is correct. Or you are at least on the right track.

Think about how the shoulders work. If someone asks you a question and you know the answer your shoulders drop and your head is effectively levitated showing confidence and comfort.

If we do not know the answer we say 'I don't know' and at the same time we perform a slight shrug our shoulders. This momentarily has the effect of lowering our head. Low confidence and discomfort.

Fixed Raised shoulders

These are a sign of low confidence. If you have ever observed a person with clinical depression you will have seen that they have a constant shrugged shoulder look about them. You can see the defeat not only in their eyes but also in their shoulders and even their movements.

In fact if we refer back to one of the first lessons, 'up is good and down is bad', we can see this in action, depressive people are never up in any sense of the word.

If this happens suddenly in reaction to stimuli it is a modified flight reaction. If is accompanied by or followed by the a comforter such as hand wringing then the person has heard or seen something that has quite literally drained him of his self confidence.

Trying to raise the shoulders enough to make the head disappear this is a sign of deep discomfort

Shrug

Shrugging the shoulders also follows the previously mentioned 'high low'. When someone gives a big shoulder shrug they are usually showing confidence in whatever they are saying.

So a statement like 'I've no idea' complete with a big shrug of the shoulders means that the person is probably telling the truth.

We can't shrug our shoulders down so the next best thing is to shrug them up as little as possible. Someone performing a small shoulder shrug and answering the question as above has does not have much confidence in what they are saying.

Single sided low shoulder shrug which is quick to come and goes a clear indicator of low confidence

A single sided shoulder shrug that is held momentarily is often a sign of distain. Try to look out for an accompanying sneer.

The same thing applies to single sided shrugs this is a low confidence sign also

Shoulder brushing

Brushing ones shoulders off as if dusting is a dismissive gesture.

If the subject does this while you are speaking to them it shows arrogance. if you could take a step back you would see that it is as if you are being symbolically swept to one side and that you are no more significant than perhaps an insect that may have landed on his shoulder.

Torso

Because the torso houses all of our vital organs the instinctive brain takes particular care of it. If there is any sign of danger or discomfort we will cover our torso and or turn away from that which is the source of the discomfort.

This covering and turning will even happen to stimuli outside the interpersonal. We do it even when watching something on the TV.

If you see a graphic surgical procedure on a TV documentary or even a soap opera we tend to cover the relative part of our own body and eventually turn away if it becomes too distressing.

Leaning

Is a good indicator of general comfort or discomfort?

Two People leaning towards each other are comfortable those that lean away are not.

If only one is leaning away then it is likely that the person has heard or seen something that has made them uncomfortable. Of course we lean away from people we do not like, sometimes almost imperceptibly

Another time one person might lean away from another is when they are showing slight deference to a superior, demonstrating that not only do they not have the right but also no intention of encroaching into their superior's personal space.

Leaning away creates distance and distancing with the body is a 'polite flight'.

The truth lean

When we are being told something that we believe to be true we tend to lean in slightly as we pay attention.

On the other hand when we are dubious or simply do not believe the information we lean away.

The opposite is true when we tell lies. In an attempt to force the person we are telling the lie to we lean forward. It is a sort of mild imposing gesture. The body also becomes compact, this creates a conspiratorial feel as if the person being told is being let into a secret.

Whilst telling the truth we will often lean back slightly. This time the lean away is a sign of confidence and comfort. It says if you don't believe me I don't care it's all I've got.

Torso Covering

Covering the torso in any way is a sign of low confidence, shutting off and comforting. It can actually progress from one to the other too. Below are just three examples.

Arm crossing

Imagine a subject with their hands crossed loosely in front of themselves this may I indicate that they are not that comfortable with the situation, or maybe they are comfortable and this is just a neutral pose for them.

Then some news is put to them which makes them feel under a little pressure, they cross or fold in an attempt to hold the information at bay.

Then more serious input is received and things get too hot to handle the hands unfold and go around the body in a self hug to comfort them.

Buttoning jacket

This can be a form of torso covering in certain situations.

I once sat and watched with interest a man at a high level meeting of about twenty executives.

During the meeting he continually buttoned and unbuttoned his jacket whilst he sat at the table. At first I thought this indicated that he had little confidence in himself or that he was undecided about the subject matter being discussed.

As I continued to observe him and look for other non verbal's, another possible explanation for his behaviour presented itself to me.

It became clear that when one particular person in the room spoke in favour of the proposals being put forward, he would unbutton his jacket.

Then when anyone spoke against the proposals he would button it back up again.

So I continued to observe, sure enough whenever positive argument was being made in regard of the subject being discussed not only did he unbutton his suit jacket but he also gave a micro nod of the head and his face was relaxed and reasonably neutral.

On the other hand when others spoke negatively he would button his jacket and display an almost imperceptible shake of the head.

Added to this a micro sneer, and I knew I was on the right track. All this was borne out later in the meeting when the voting took place.

Interestingly at the very end of this meeting the chairman stood to announce his opinion, as he did so he slowly and deliberately closed and buttoned his suit jacket.

This was to let everyone in the meeting know that whatever he was about to say was final and that he was now closed off to all conversation, also that the meeting was about to close.

So you can see that people at this meeting were using their jackets as extensions of their body in order to display body language.

With an object

This can be placing objects on a table to form a barrier, it doesn't have to be a large object since the effect is psychological a pencil or pen will do the trick. It can also be something more substantial.

I once had an issue with one of my son, nothing serious I hasten to add, the usual domestic stuff probably about something having been broken I really don't remember.

I do, though, remember the non verbal behaviour which he displayed at the time. I asked him to sit on the sofa. He was obviously aware that there was an issue, because as he sat he picked up a throw cushion and held it on his lap in front of him, when I started to talk to him about things that were concerning me the pillow slowly but surely came off his lap and across his chest.

When I reached the critical point and asked him a direct question he pulled the cushion tight and started to rub his chin on it.

You see he started with an initial low confidence barrier on his lap.

Then he moved to a shut out pose with the cushion on his chest.

Finally on to an all out comforter as he moved it to under his chin, or in front of his neck dimple to be precise.

Alpha male

Taking up space with the torso when standing or sitting is a territorial display. This will be discussed more in the hands and leg section of this book.

Puffing up of the chest is a dominance display often seen in police officers along with the elbows flared out to the sides; it is a display of authority.

Notice how police officers also walk or stand with their legs and feet at shoulder width Notice how when they do this their thumbs are kept out of sight in their stab vests. This allows them to take a dominant stance but at the same time minimise any overt display of aggression.

This pose is not just copied from one officer to the next. This pose is actually taught to them.

In future you can watch out for this it is almost comical if you have a chance to see several police officers on patrol at an event such as a county fair.

When you see two of them speaking to each other face to face the pose is easy to spot as being manufactured rather than natural.

Towards and away

When comfortable we are happy to face another person. After all you are psychologically exposing your vital organs to that person

Having the torso facing away from someone can mean lots of things. The underlying signal is that they do not feel comfortable.

It is of course a distancing pose keeping the vital organs facing away from that which is not liked or trusted.

It is often seen along with backward movement.

Sometimes an intention pose showing the subject is about to, or would prefer to, leave. The intention can be easier seen when the feet face the same direction as the torso.

We also try to diminish the size of our body when it is under threat. We attempt to make as small a target as possible.

Later you will read about males framing and pointing to their genitals as a form of attracting women. Women do a similar thing to attract men they lift the top of their body upwards as if taking and holding a deep breath quite literally showing off their breasts.

This pose only happens if the woman is reasonably confident in herself or that her intended target is already somewhat interested in her.

Arms

We use our arms for so many things we wave them in recognition and to attract attention. We move them around when we speak in order to be more expressive. We put them up to protect ourselves in times of danger.

We need to look at this last part of the above statement in more detail in order to understand the significance of arm positioning from the point of non verbals.

Inner Outer

The inside of the forearms and biceps are quite soft and vulnerable compared to the outside of the forearm and the triceps.

If we are in the company of loved ones and friends our arms are open to them allowing access to the 'inner' arms. If however something like an errant football were to come flying towards our face, we would put our arm up in front of ourselves with the 'outer' arm facing the danger.

So showing the inner arms is a sign of comfort, while when uncomfortable we face our outer arms in that direction.

Crossed arms can mean many things such as torso covering and self hugging both discussed in the previous section. Most of you will be familiar with the idea that crossed arms are sign of being shut off.

Frozen arms

When the arms literally freeze and are held close down beside the body it is the ultimate discomfort sign.

It's as if we are saying no matter what happens I am not able to defend, pacify or comfort myself. Frozen arms are the arms of the defeated.

Wide arms

Spreading out of the arms is territorial display similar to the police officer example discussed above.

Whenever this is seen on a table or similar it is a territorial display.

In fact the wider the arms the more confident or even aggressive the subject is being. It is the dominant gorilla pose.

Arm movement

Arm movement is used to augment the spoken message. Moving the arms around helps to express and exaggerate visually what is being said.

Remember how we say something is more important than what is actually said well the arms come into play here too. If we are explaining something to someone a, big project or a large object for instance, we demonstrate with wide and high arms.

The same goes for if we are comfortable or confident the arm movements reflect this.

When we are low in confidence or are not so comfortable then our arm movements will be less expressive.

When someone's arm movements are smaller or generally more diminished than usual then there is a problem. Remember baseline.

If you see a change from big arm movements to smaller ones during the course of an interaction then the confidence has been diminished.

this diminishing in confidence could be in response to input or indeed as a result of there being less confidence in our own output in other words what we are saying we may not have complete confidence in. Could you have just been told a lie?

I was once attending a training course. I and the other students had gathered in the lobby waiting for the lecturer.

We all knew the lecturer reasonably well and so he felt very comfortable around us, and we around him, like all good teachers he had a great sense of humour. It was the second day of the course and as soon as he arrived he did what is known as the look forward.

So during his look forward to the timetable for the day ahead he was moving his arms around in big movements trying to create some excitement.

He was showing us a lot of inner arm. When he said to us that we were about to start and that we were to follow him to the Sherwood rooms his arm was up at shoulder level again inner arm exposed.

One of the students, a practical joker, asked him if he was sure that was the correct room since she had seen another large group in their watching a slide show as she'd passed earlier.

Immediately the lecturers arm dropped to his side and even his shoulders slumped. After a second or two he puffed his cheeks and breathed out. He started to turn very slowly. He was obviously considering all the implications of the room having been double booked.

In half a second he went from being an excited in control confident man to looking like a small child.

Just as he was about to head off to the reception he asked the woman 'are you sure?' she smiled and said 'gotcha!' his relief was evident, he turned to her and shook his fist, outer arm showing, with a wry smile on his face.

Interestingly in the split second that the student announced her little joke a micro expression of a contempt sneer appeared on the lecturers face.

At the end of the course she was the only one held back, I was later told that she had failed one of her practical assessments!

So the lecturer went from confidence to no confidence to defiance in seconds and at no time did his voice change in tone. All these emotions were shown by his arm movements alone.

Hands

These are the dextrous tools of the body, they perform so many tasks for us, and they are a truly remarkable thing.

They can thread a needle, form a fist and punch, caress a lover or strangle the very life from someone.

Hands are very expressive part of the body we use them to convey messages both unconsciously and consciously.

First we will look at larger movements and work our way down to the smaller more subtle ones. The hands help to express the spoken word and are just as important in getting the message across, obviously used in conjunction with the arms as discussed previously.

Stay away

Hands held up in front of ourselves, fingers pointing up and palms out is an overt gesture to stay away or I don't like you or what you are saying/ doing.

We do this consciously to let others know we don't want them to come near or even not to say something.

We also make this gesture unconsciously and often in far smaller movements. If we have our hands resting on a table or in our lap and we hear something we don't like we tend to raise our hands ever so slightly sometimes even keeping our wrists planted, just like the large overt movement we are saying I'm not comfortable please keep that away from me.

A good example of how this works is if we are offered something. We use our hands to convey the conviction of our verbal statement. I have seen informal events and noted with amusement how various exchanges evolve according to body language even when the spoken message is identical.

A dozen people sitting at a barbecue and the host circulates offering hotdogs to his guests. If a person politely refuses with their hands out in front of them in the 'stay away gesture' the host accepts this and moves on.

If he offers someone else a hotdog and they refuse without any hand gesture the host will almost certainly ask if he is sure or try to persuade him. Watch this interaction it is irrefutable proof that body language is more powerful than the spoken word.

Another keep away gesture is actually the opposite physically and the message is even more powerful.

This is when we hold our hands behind our back. This is a very strong unmistakable message of I am completely unapproachable except in a very formal way I Will not allow my space to be encroached upon.

Imagine your child came to you for a hug and you kept your hands behind your back, the message would be both unmistakable and devastating to the child.

Putting your hands behind your back says don't come close but instead of in a defensive pose it is a pose of absolute authority.

This is the pose of the most powerful and confident among us, since the torso is exposed and the potentially protective arms are nowhere to be seen.

Hands on hips

Hands on hips with the thumbs forward show an open enquiring stance. Although the thumbs are showing they are of little significance when it comes to hands on hips. In this instance the direction of the fingers is the telling read.

Fingers facing backwards are less confident often signifying that someone is being inquisitive. It is more to do with how the arms tend to point backwards and away than the hand display.

When the fingers face forward this is a more confident pose. It can even display a feeling of dominance or aggression this has more to do with the pointed brackets effect of the arms than the hands.

Hands on hips thumbs facing back is a dominant sometimes even aggressive stance

Interlaced hands

A hand interlaced placed behind the head is a high confidence stance. Much like the pointed bracket appearance of the arms it is a high confidence space taking pose.

It says I am the best in the room. In fact when you see this in a meeting it will usually only be displayed by one person and that one person will always be the leader.

The only time you will see this display by more than one person is in a social setting when two highly comfortable people are mirroring each other.

Interlaced hands as in a closed prayer are a sign of low confidence. Having the palms touching like this is a comforter and the position actually mimics a person in prayer which is a submissive pose.

Interlaced hands that are making a wringing motion go beyond low confidence to stress. It changes from an indicator to a comforter.

This also applies to rubbing hands together or rubbing the fingers of one hand across the palm or back of the other.

Of course as with all body language there are exceptions, Women sometimes show interest in a man by gently scratching or stroking the back of one hand.

This is a primitive gesture, she is subconsciously sending a message to the man that she would like to be groomed just like a chimpanzee in the jungle

Steeple

We know of course that up is good. When it comes to the hands it is no different. There is a pose which shows us that up is not just good but up is best.

The most confident of all non verbal gestures is when we mimic a church steeple with our hands and fingers; in fact this hand gesture is called 'the steeple'.

The finger tips touch but the palms do not. They are also spread out. If the elbows remain at waist high the steeple is exaggerated and becomes a steeple from elbow to fingertips.

A modified steeple is when the hands are interlaced but the forefingers are not. They point up and touch to form the steeple.

Watch a television interview where the interviewee starts out confident, see the steeple as they smile and are cordial; of course they are confident and comfortable.

Then watch for the change. As the questions become more difficult the fingers go from touching at the tip to interlacing then onto a full hand interlace they may even move on to display some hand wringing.

Hidden hands

This is a very negative gesture unless it is displayed by someone in authority as discussed in hands behind the back.

If your hands are invisible either behind your back under a table or in your pockets you will be perceived as being dishonest even though it may not be true.

As for having your hands in your pockets this is still seen by many as a disrespectful pose.

If you remember from early on in the book we like to see ourselves in others and we are always looking for congruence. So you see if subject's hands are in their pockets and the readers are not there can be no mirroring.

Also we like to see the hands and arms move in unison with the lips as discussed before. Put these facts together and we see why we do not like to see subjects with their hands in their pockets.

Hidden hands can be coy, women will hold their hands behind their backs in order to show they willing to be vulnerable and if accompanied by torso swinging it is totally submissive and a flirting gesture which cannot be misunderstood.

Applauding

This is a very noisy affair and is not conducive with hiding our emotional state or being a shrinking violet.

This activity can range from slow hand clapping as a disrespectful gesture of impatience to vigorous appreciative hand clapping, sometimes this can even turn into table banging to increase the effect

Hand clapping over the head in victory. I see this every week at the end of a football game. The head is held up and the arms are just about as high as they can go.

The winning team will do this without fail. The only exception I have witnessed to this was once when my team won by such a huge margin that they were embarrassed for the other team and the hand clapping was much lower than usual

Hand clapping over the head in defeat. This is almost identical only the head will be dropped. Again a losing team will go to their fans and do the overhead clap in an apologetic manner.

Palms

As with all parts of the body we have a tough and a delicate side. When it comes to hands it's the palms that are the delicate side and it shows in how we display them.

Palms up

With the arms out in front of us at ninety degrees to the body elbows at waste high if the palms face up they are confident and open. They are inviting others into either our space or into an idea if we are speaking. Often there will be a slight up and down motion of the arms. It looks like the subject is gently juggling a ball in their hands. If you want people to listen keep the palms up.

A variation on the palms up is when they remain exposed and the arms drop below the horizontal. This is a deliberate showing of vulnerability. The subject's hands are literally pleading with you.

Palms down

The arms in the same position as above but with the palms facing down is of course the opposite we are being told there is no room for discussion. If you have been conversing with this person then it is over.

If the hands are turned so that the palms face away from us this is very significant. Obviously they form a barrier but also this gesture can be used to try and force the spoken word in your direction.

It says you must accept what I am saying. So you can see that this is an odd gesture to use if trying to convince someone of the truthfulness of a statement.

Palms facing in

If the palms face the subject it is a sign of quiet confidence. This also goes for when one hand is cupped in the other and passive.

Shaking hands

Means we are nervous, some caution is stressed here though, there are those that naturally have trembling hands so this is a must see in the setting of a baseline.

Also over excitement can cause the hands to tremble, as with all observations they must be read in context

Handshake

Whole books have been written about handshakes so many in fact that it would seem trite to try to cover the whole subject in this one however there are some fundamentals worth looking at.

The person who offers the hand first is either in control or subservient, of course as with all tells the handshake must be taken in context and along with other reads.

Strong

The stronger the handshake the more powerful the subject is, or at least, perceives themselves to be.

Bear in mind that this may be the only time the two of you are in this close a proximity some people take the opportunity to big themselves up.

I have had very firm handshakes from people in the past only to see them wilt during a meeting under even the slightest pressure.

Some domineering folk will attempt to have their hand on top during a handshake. The hand is not actually on top it's just that their palm faces ever so slightly down asserting their status.

I once read an article advising people on the receiving end of such a handshake to actually twist their hands to the top and squeeze as hard as they could.

I've never seen it attempted but can you imagine a handshake between two people if they had both read the same book.

Weak

It follows then that the weaker the handshake the more subservient or weaker the person.

This also is only partially true. I have a family member who is a politician and when we greet our handshake is really quite ordinary. I have seen this family member on the campaign trail and it is quite apparent that weakness is not one of his attributes.

A variation on the weak handshake is the light handshake reserved by men for women usually in social settings.

In the workplace women shake hands on an equal footing. So it is usually firmer however still not domineering

Incidentally in the work environment if a woman offers here hand in to a man first then she sees herself as in control.

Waving hands

When it comes to hands being used in greetings and farewells the higher the hand is held the more positive the emotion behind it. High waving hands are excited and pleased.

Waves from the hip are almost dismissive and are not genuinely warm. So the lower down the wave goes the less respect and or friendship exists between the communicating couple.

Fists

When we make fist with our hand or hands it is a sign of strength, this show of strength is universal regardless of the situation.

The shaking of the fist up in front of the face is saying I am the one. This is true, I am a winner. I am willing to meet you head on.

If we make a fist with our hands at our side this is a sure indicator that we are moving to the fight state. We have been angered and have had enough

A fist banged on a table or a lectern is saying I believe and so should you.

When both hands are clenched and then raised above the head this is the universal signal that a victory has been achieved.

Hands on knees

When the person you are talking to moves forward in their seat and puts both hands on their knees they are telling you that they are leaving, right now.

They will often cut in and say something akin to 'much as I'd like to hear what you have to say I really must be going'.

If you are in a power play of some sort such as a negotiation and you see this lean, you can take charge before they speak by being dismissive of them.

I have done this myself. Just as my adversary in a meeting lent forward and put his hands on his knees I stood looked at my watch and made a half apology and told him I had to be somewhere important.

He was immediately put on the back foot (freeze) and it put me in control.

Hands that stay on knees for a long time is a sign of low confidence especially if the hands cup the knees and the person is leaning forward.

Putting our hands on property can be done to show ownership. It is amusing to observe in young males. They seem to be permanently touching their cars and their girlfriends.

Fingers and Thumbs

Quite a bit of finger posing and movement is covered in the previous section because some hand movement and poses incorporate the fingers. I am not going to repeat the facts. Instead read back over hands once you have finished the section on fingers and thumbs.

Biting your nails overtly in front of others will be read as a sign of low confidence. It is about an inch away from sucking your thumb which is the mother of all comforting behaviours. Thumb sucking starts with new born babies and needs no external triggers or encouragement from adults.

Finger pointing especially if it is accompanied by waging is a universal insult it shows disrespect and arrogance

This is also true of finger clicking when directed at others to gain their attention.

When we put our fingers on top of a surface like a desk and our palms are raised, in a sort of giant spider pose, it is a display of confidence. Subjects will often push their weight forward in this position trying to force an issue.

If this pose turns to finger drumming it is a sign of impatience and even anger

A similar stance to this is when the fingers are parted only very slightly this is a neutral or quietly confident.

If this turns to drumming fingers is a sure sign of nervousness

Picking at the fingers with the thumb on the same hand shows that a subject is bored. Not only bored but they are also keen to let you know they are bored

Thumbs

Although one of the smallest individual appendages they can carry very powerful non verbal messages. Apart from the very obvious and mostly conscious signals of thumbs up and thumbs down.

Thumbs up show confidence

Thumbs down is a sign that this person lacks confidence

Turning the thumb to the side with the rest of your fingers in the clenched position is dismissive and offensive. It is the same gesture we use to thumb a lift at the side of the road.

When we direct it at a person it is the high of rudeness beyond finger pointing.

Hidden thumbs are showing that the person is at a very low point on the confidence scale. Those with clinical depression often hide their thumbs in many different ways.

Hidden thumbs such as when they are put into pockets and the fingers are still on display is a sign of low confidence.

The opposite where the fingers are placed in the pockets and the thumbs are still visible is a high confidence indicator.

There is an exception to hidden thumbs being low confidence and this is during genital framing. Which you will read about in the next chapter.

The Bottom

Genitals

A very delicate part of the anatomy of course, especially for male, but also quite prominent, or rather exposed. They are all out in front unlike other organs which are encased and protected.

Protecting

Covering the genital area is a protective act. In fact it is such a sensitive area both physically and for the instinctive system covering the genitals is often done overtly and quite unashamedly.

This of course makes sense to the all our brains from the unconscious through the subconscious right up to the conscious.

Sometimes when the stimuli become so vivid and worrying to the subject, they can often be seen to, not only cover, but actually apply pressure in that area in an attempt at the ultimate protection.

It's as if they are trying to force the genitals back inside the body. The face of the person will often contort as if in real agony accompanied by very real gasping sounds. Interestingly the younger adult males among us will react more strongly than older men.

Framing

Having the hands form a frame around the genitals is a high confidence indicator. Associated with preliminary courting.

Men will often stand at a bar facing females with their hands facing downwards and inwards. It is an attempt to draw attention to the genitals in a peacock like display.

Having their thumbs in the pockets and the fingers pointing towards the genitals is a similar sign. It is actually an attempt to draw the eyes to that region.

When seated men will often frame the genitals by having their legs akimbo and leaning forward allowing their hands to dangle between their legs and their wrists to frame the genitals. There is no mistaking this as a modification of the above mating gesture.

Legs

Legs are our largest limbs and are responsible for moving us from one place to another. They are very good indicators of the overall mood and intention of the subject.

These are the things that will stop and freeze mid stride when alerted.

They will literally facilitate flight and of course if we are forced to fight they hold us firm and steady.

Legs are not to be ignored.

Leg rubbing

A universal comforter, it is one of the most highly reliable indicators of stress. It not only comforts but also is an unconscious effort to 'shoo' away the stimuli which is causing the discomfort.

We rub down our thighs especially when sitting, almost as if we are pushing the undesirable information away from our bodies and back in the direction it came from.

Superior leg rub

Watch out too for the superior leg rub. The subject will slowly rub the thigh as they talk, if the legs are crossed it will be the top leg, with confidence or in a condescending manner often the facial sneer will be present as one or more micro expressions during the exchange.

This leg rubbing can become even more pronounced and actually lead to leg preening which is the ultimate dismissal of the other person.

This leg preening, identical to the shoulder preen mentioned earlier, looks for all to see as if we are literally picking minute bits of dirt off our leg and throwing them off. It says you are no more than a piece of dirt and I am not listening.

Leg crossing, seated.

Have both negative and positive connotations. The clue is to look at the posture of the rest of the body and facial expression but as a general rule here's how the crossed leg sends a message.

If the leg is crossed towards you, that is to say that, the foot of the top leg is facing you this is a comfort signal and things are probably fine.

When the top leg faces away then the opposite is true, the thigh is attempting to form a barrier between the two of you.

If someone crosses their legs unnaturally high and even puts their hands around their shin and thigh this is asserting the barrier and making it appear immovable.

There is no getting through to this person.

Leg crossing, standing

When legs are crossed and we are standing we are showing a very high degree of comfort and confidence. Having crossed legs while standing means our guard is completely down since it is so incongruent with being able to flee if danger should present itself.

By crossing one leg over the other you are supporting your whole weight on one leg.

Try this, it is fun and it works. Next time you are at a party or gathering wait until people have relaxed enough that several are standing with their legs crossed and having a good time, pick an opportune moment and make a loud crashing sound.

Drop a tray or similar and watch. The reaction to the fright will be one of two things. First they may immediately uncross their legs and put themselves' back on an even footing and freeze, or they will simply freeze momentarily before slowly uncrossing their legs. They will immediately follow this with a comforter.

Leg movements

Twitching, bouncing, swinging legs are all signs of a basic discomfort. It can occur when standing or seated with feet planted or crossed.

Because of the legs function they only really have a couple of messages to send.

Get me out of here or stand and fight.

So once you see the legs move watch out for other clues and you will be able to see what the subject intentions are.

Beware; leg movement in the form of twitching, bouncing etc can also indicate excitement. In extreme cases it will turn into jumping about.

Twitching.

General small twitching of the legs can very often be a nervous habit but of course this will be identified during the baseline observations.

If however twitching is not a continuous behaviour and it occurs it can indicate that the subject has become uncomfortable. The message is I no longer want to be here.

The reason for the discomfort will need to be established is it because they have heard or seen something they didn't like or is it just general impatience.

Bouncing legs

A more pronounced form of twitching. So of course it can indicate the same flight intention just with a greater degree of discomfort.

When seated we often see a pronounced leg bouncing motion. Of course it is signifying discomfort but the intention is slightly different from above. This time it is an aggressive movement it is a instinctive kick.

We are attempting to kick away information or even symbolically kick out at someone or something. When our legs bounce it is the final defence mechanism 'kicking in', excuse the pun.

When flirting women can often be seen bouncing or swinging their legs

Wide legs

Wide legs are territorial claims. Taking up space especially at the expense of others is a dominating pose; it says I am more important than you.

Often this is done quite consciously with a projected pretence that the subject themselves are unaware of their own encroachments.

If it occurs face to face whilst standing it can be more than just dominance being displayed. Along with knotted brows and folded arms it can be a very aggressive stance. This is an attempt to make ourselves more stable and ready for combat.

Feet

Because the feet have such an important job to do in the fright to fight process they should be observed in as much detail as is practicably possible.

Ultimately along with the legs these are the things that will either carry you away to safety during the flight or keep your legs upright and steady if it comes to fight. So when it comes to reading the feet know this that **they cannot deceive**. The feet show emotion and intention in real time reacting instantly to stimuli.

Facing feet

Feet face where they want to be. Watch two lovers kissing or dancing and their feet will not only be facing each other but also intertwined.

Feet facing away are a sign of discomfort in some way.

The feet point to where they want to go, even if the operator of them has to stay. If you are talking to someone and one of their feet is facing the door then they are showing their intention and impatient to leave.

If both feet are facing the door and only their upper body is facing you then they have already dismissed you none verbally and are probably not walking due to social convention. Feet facing away are ultimately saying I don't want to be here

Dancing feet

Dancing is a universal expression of joy. Adjusted dancing or dumbed down dancing in the interests of social etiquette are therefore signs of comfort.

This can mean anything from toes curling up, or gleeful jiggling of feet to standing on tiptoe to give oneself that ten feet tall feeling. This can be going even further. Jumping for joy.

Toes pointing up are a happy gesture it is a conservative version of dancing or jumping. Often seen when seated.

I recently saw two women in a coffee shop; they were leaning in and talking happily maybe in a slightly conspiratorial way.

During the conversation one woman was rotating her foot around slowly while the other woman spoke. Suddenly her foot stopped and curled up toes pointing to the ceiling.

I said to my son who was drinking with me 'that woman over there is about to laugh'. Sure enough within seconds she started to laugh out load.

What had happened? Well she was showing intrigue but not only by leaning in also because her foot was slowly rotating while she absorbed information which was inoffensive, then when the toes went up it was in anticipation of a punch line of some sort.

Planted feet

Frozen feet are unhappy feet they can indicate the freeze response; they can also be the planted feet of the intention to fight.

In both cases the accompanying emotion is one of discomfort. They are also 'down feet' I refer of course to up is good and down bad. Since we can't actually push our feet down through the floor we show low feelings by gluing our feet to it

When we are sure of ourselves and we are standing our feet tend to be directly beneath our shoulders, for men at least. When we are less than comfortable our feet tend to get closer together. For women this is not necessarily the case especially if wearing a skirt or dress.

Hidden feet

Are a sure sign of discomfort and low confidence, as mentioned in all other areas of the body any movement one subject makes away from another, or object, is an attempt to put distance between them? If this happens suddenly then it is a sure sign of negative reaction.

Twitching, bouncing or swinging feet is covered above in the legs section

Shuffling feet

Discomfort or impatience. This is like a sort of walking on the spot the instinctive brain is carrying out the motion without taking us anywhere.

I see this with children when they are being chastised along with the previously discussed dropped head they shuffle their feet. Obviously they would rather be anywhere else than here right now.

Dangling shoe.

Women often do this as a high comfort pose. They have their heal exposed and the shoe just hangs on their toes often accompanied by foot movement. If things take a turn in any negative direction the shoe goes straight back on.

Tonality

How we say something accounts for thirty eight percent of getting the message across to others. Obviously it is not as important as our actual body language but vastly more important that the actual words leaving our mouth. In fact over five times more important and therefore five times more honest.

Reading this non verbal indicator is almost as important as the body language, especially if the person delivering the message is adept at masking and the reader is not quick enough to see or correctly decipher the micro expressions being given

First thing to note is does the verbal delivery have congruence with the body language and the actual words being spoken.

Is the verbal message one of calm, if so does the voice sound calm and even? Is it quite neutral compared to the normal 'benchmarked' speech of the subject?

If the message is one of excitement, good news or a surprise. Does the tonality match? And also are their matching body expressions.

Remember if exciting news is being given. The body should be on the up. The facial expression should be happy and the tone excited. Also arm movements in particular should be expressive.

Deceit

Is someone lying to me?

I have put just a short chapter in here for the human polygraph enthusiasts. It is only a short chapter because to do the subject justice needs a whole book.

A word of warning though. Detecting lies is a very difficult skill is careful not to too easily judge others.

Detecting lies is the hardest part of non verbal reading. Tests have shown that even the best in the world have only a fifty-fifty success rate when it comes to being a human polygraph.

When trying to look for lies we must be circumspect and rely on multiple reads it is not a quick or easy thing. It becomes easier depending on how close a relationship we have with the subject. As I mention before parents are good lie detectors but even then only to a point.

If you choose to use your non verbal skills to detect lies then you must have a very solid baseline. You must become super efficient at reading all aspects of the Tells you read. One tells on its own will give you nothing.

Bear in mind that what we are looking for overall is discomfort. The problem lies right there when we put someone under pressure the process itself is unsettling. Also the nature of the questioning could be aggressive and cause discomfort in itself.

The first and most important thing to remember if you intend to question someone is to remain calm.

The next is exactly the same as the first advice in this book and that is to establish a reliable benchmark. Make sure you know the neutral or comfortable habits of the subject. This has to be done over time the longer the better. Ask inane questions, as many as it takes before moving on.

Once you are certain you have a reliable bench mark ask more probing questions before moving on to the damning ones.

Although there is no scientific order to the non verbal response system below is not a bad logical pattern. Following on from the Fright, Freeze Flight, Fight system you can expect to see this show up in a mini version in the tells.

Ask the question clearly and pause

Look for a micro expression first remember these are true tells

Then notice any changes no matter how slight to posture facial expression or other movement

Finally watch out for a comforter.

If you noticed anything which alerts you, pursue this line of questioning. And repeat the process remember to remain calm.

When people tell the truth they tend to reinforce their verbal's with expressive movements.

For example if they say to the right. They will point or nod their head to their right. When people are telling lies these movements become far less prevalent.

Sometimes nonexistent. Watch out though a good liar will over emphasise in an attempt to trick your instinctive brain into seeing the wrong body language. The rule is that accompanying expressions should reinforce the spoken work but not be forced.

Another thing that happens when people lie is that the stress tends to tighten the vocal chords. Their voice can become flatter than usual.

The actual answers will become less expressive too. Especially if the baseline is for a person to be a chatterbox, then suddenly under questioning they revert to short answers. In the extreme just yes or no.

Liars tend to pacify after making untrue statements. This is generally associated with lies of commission. These are lies where the subject has made an untrue declaration

Also the tongue poke is a classic indicator of lying. This usually accompanies a lie of omission. These are lies where information is withheld.

The tongue poke can also be an indicator of the subject not wanting to talk too.

It is worth repeating again and again. Benchmark and look for multiple reads.

Beautiful Game

I have included this chapter as a sort of example of how easy it is to see body language all around us all the time and ignore it.

Every week I go to see my local football (soccer) team.

Every week I watch a series of dances between the players the officials and the crowd.

The relationship between the three elements is fascinating. The mood of the crowd affects the players. The player's performance affects the crowd. The officials are supposed to be even handed parental figures ensuring fair play. This all sounds very obvious but take a closer look.

The yellow card

A foul is committed and the referee blows his whistle. The offending player nearly always walks away from the incident and the ref. Although players are told to do this there is also an underlying instinctive element to this. He is making an attempt to distance himself from the threat.

The crowd as this point begins to shout at the referee this is a universal protection response.

The referee moves towards the player gets out his yellow card and shows it to the player.

At this point it gets real interesting, on nearly every occasion the player will turn his back on the referee and bend down. Most often he will make a show of pulling up his socks. What he is actually doing is showing the ref his rear end.

The player will then either walk away or go to the opposition man he fouled and shake hands. This is a good indicator of the general atmosphere that the game is being played in.

Another thing was happening here too the referee was allowing all and sundry to see just how much authority he has over the game in general too.

When he moved towards the player he was indicating willingness to compromise by having to chase the player onto his piece of turf.

And by allowing the player to face away from him and have to show the card to his back again says that the player is in charge.

A referee in full control of the match will stop still where the incident took place and make the offender come back to him and show the card to his face. As the player turns to carry out the ritual bending over the ref should turn away.

The red card

Again the ref blows his whistle.

This time however the foul is a serious one. The offending player knows this. Unlike the yellow card incident the player will stand his ground. He knows flight will not work.

He moves straight onto fight. He stands his ground, he suspects that the consequence of his actions may be severe and so he prepares to argue his case usually very expressively.

The ref comes over and shows the red card.

Now the player knows there is no going back however he still protests. The protests now are for a different reason. The full impact of the situation comes to him. He knows he has let his team and supporters down.

He also knows he is going to have the walk of shame off the field. The further away from the pitch exit he is the longer he will protest.

In this instance the referee is right to go to the player. This shows authority and intent. He knows that if he allows the player to come to him it would be unduly cruel. This is akin to a parent going straight to a child to smack him for unacceptable behaviour. Rather than making the child suffers by walking to his own fate.

The crowd's reaction initially is the same as the yellow card. They will defend their own at any cost. This turns to a nervous silence as they realise their team is weakened.

Also the perceived honesty of the player is expressed by how the crowd reacts generally.

If the player is seen to be a fair minded and hard working member of the team he will be applauded by a large part of the crowd, this applause maybe muted but it will follow him right off the pitch.

His offence is seen as out of character and possibly even a genuine mistake.

If the player is one who seems to always be a bit on the overly aggressive side or he is a gambler then the applause will be non existent. If there is any at all it will be from a few fans only, those will be the ones who like his throwback style.

Twelfth man.

When the crowd is buoyant this spills onto the field of play. They chant and encourage the players individually and as a team. They stamp and clap. All these things are UP. Making noise is a positive thing.

The players respond because they are being made to feel good about themselves. Their heads are held up and they make effort in their tackling and running. They are also willing to try daring things.

This has a snowball affect the players try hard the crowd appreciates the effort and encourages more. And this goes on and on. The team usually have a good result on a day like this.

Even if the team do not win the effort is appreciated and the players appreciate the support.

This circle of events can begin with either. It can start with one small piece of good play which gets the crowd into the positive mood. Or, interestingly, it can start with the crowd being in good spirits to begin with.

Most people think that the crowd is either being the twelfth man or nothing. This couldn't be further from the truth. The crowd and the team are connected.

So the relationship can either be positive or negative but it cannot be nothing. So the crowd is either helping or hindering

The Achilles heal

The opposite of the twelfth man effect is when the emotion spirals in the opposite direction. If the crowd is quite it can make it difficult for the team. If they are critical this can spell disaster.

Again this can start with the players or the spectators.

If a player makes a bad move say a wayward pass early in the game he is forgiven. He is still encouraged for his vision and effort. If he or other players make many more then watch out. The forgiveness can turn to some impatient groans. Then worse, criticism!

Once there is criticism it's all over. The players have no choice but to respond in kind. Remember the instinctive brain makes the real decision.

The players will take up less space as they shrink slightly. They become less willing to try their hardest. And they certainly won't take risks.

This then leads to them panicking when they're on the ball or even over thinking.

The unconscious either says kick the ball (the responsibility) as far away as possible. Or they take the extra half a second deciding in an effort not to make the mistake. The other team maintains its pace and appears to be quicker and better.

Of course the crowd then becomes more critical and the whole thing gets worse.

The super sub

The trouble is the crowd and the team are now in a rut.

Changing the tone to upbeat is almost impossible. Unless something inspirational happens.

Like a goal out of the blue. Or the arrival of the proverbial super sub.

The super sub phenomenon is quite something. This player arrives after having witnessed the negative vibe. His team mates are in a rut and so are the crowd. He has nothing to loose and will not be judged as harshly as the rest since he was not present during the initial crisis. *

His arrival allows for a couple of things to happen.

An injection of energy and for the crowd to reset its mood.

The sub arrives with instructions to the team to up their game and make the effort.

The crowd thinks it can't get worse. This is critical. Because they think it can't get worse they must be unconsciously thinking it can only improve. It can't stay exactly the same because the makeup of the team has changed.

So as the game restarts the elements of the crowd will shout encouragement and the team spirit is lifted slightly, it's a new beginning.

Before you know it the game is turned on its head. The players are performing better and the crowd is chanting and encouraging.

Subs can change everything especially if the player is liked by the crowd and respected by his peers.

Incidentally the player being replaced has a lot to say with his body too. If he is being replaced due to injury he will usually hobble off. Prior to coming off though he sometimes plays a game of cat and mouse.

If his team are in the lead he will walk to the other side of the pitch in order to have a longer walk to leave the field by the officials. And he will walk as if drained of enough energy to even break into a jog.

If however the team is losing we will see him run off the pitch to enable a quick as possible turnaround.

If a player is substituted against his will for tactical advantage for instance they will often be displeased. Putting their arms down and palms forward in a questioning gesture.

He knows why he is being replaced he just wants the crowd to see that he is unhappy without being openly insubordinate to the manager.

Goal for

When my team score a goal. The reaction by everyone is the same

The first second as the ball goes in the net is pure instinct. Arms go up people jump up the player jumps and stretch his arms in the air. Everyone supporters and players alike are caught up in the euphoria.

This is what it is all about.

Remember everything is UP and up is good.

Interestingly after the initial celebration the players particularly the ones directly involved in scoring will applaud the crowd.

This is often misinterpreted as a sign that the players are dedicating the goal to everyone. Actually they are thanking the crowd for their part in the goal. The positives of being the twelfth man one of the players.

They are indicating instinctively we are all in the team.

GOAL AGAINST

When a goal is scored against us this is obviously bad

The crowd is stunned into silence and the mood is dark.

But watch the players for an indication of how the rest of the game will go.

We use an expression 'their heads have dropped' and this is more than just an expression.

The player's heads will actually go down. Their shoulders slump and their body movements become lethargic. Not to the point that they are moping around but it's there.

Sometimes the goal is against the run of play and this actually can have the opposite effect on the players.

The injustice makes them redouble their efforts they keep their heads up the crowd continue to encourage and they carry on playing well. This often results in a quick equalizer.

This is also attributable to the fact that the teams that have just scored become vulnerable. Their limbic or instinctive brain has just achieved a target and for a minute or two they are still experiencing that feeling of achievement.

It is not such an easy thing to set you a new goal so soon after just achieving one.

On the Attack

This really is the instinctive animal at work.

A team on the attack becomes the predators. On the ball they tease run stop looking constantly for away to move in and kill (well beat anyway) the opponent directly in front of them.

The other players in his team are trying to get an advantage of course.

Their heads bob around. Their body movement is aggressive and upbeat.

In defence

The defensive team is backing away. Signs of flight. Until they get near their own nest or goal. Then they stand their ground ready to fight. They make their bodies big in an attempt to show dominance.

Once they know they are committed to fight, then tackle for the ball.

Race with the opponent in order to force them away from goal.

And there is usually a whole lot of pushing and shoving going on

Of course all of these things are part of the plan the tactics and so forth but it is interesting that a lot of the stuff which happens is instinctive and is displayed in the body language.

One of the biggest criticisms I hear is that players ball watch. Try not to be too harsh on them this is the classic freeze. For a split second their brain recognizes that there is a threat and the instinctive thing for the body to do is freeze. How long the freeze is held is usually the critical thing.

I mentioned in an earlier chapter winning and losing so will not repeat it. What I will mention is that these observations are made by myself in the flesh so to speak every week. The team I support, cheer and love is Boston United.

Thanks for reading my book. Please visit Amazon.com or Amazon.co.uk and leave feedback

Also check out my other titles all available at Amazon.

Join the Dots.

Instant Hypnosis Exposed.

Waking Self Hypnosis.

Speed hypnosis in Therapy.

Stories that Heal.